From The Women's Press Ltd
124 Shoreditch High Street, London E1

D1927686

Contributors:

Naomi Alexander
Annalou
Renée d'Arcy
Ros Asquith
Ann Barefoot
Sue Beasley
Carey Bennet
Laetitia Bermejo
Helen Chadwick
Kate Charlsworth
Helen Cherry
Sally Corless
Hilary Driver
Riana Duncan
Mary Ellis
Diane Fisher
Jacky Fleming
Wanda Gorzgowska
Sophie Grillet
Linda Harding
Jo Harvatt
Julie Hoehn
Caroline Holden
June Huckerby
Cath Jackson
Marie-Hélène Jeeves
Mishelle Jones
Kathryn Lamb
Christine Landreth
Annie Lawson
Name mislaid. Apologies.
Jan Lewis
Maggie Ling
Marian Lydbrooke
Margaret Maidment
Angela Martin
Paloma Massip-Pozo
Lyn May
Alison McEwan
Jean Meyer
Carel Moiseiwitsch
Bridget Moore
Stefy Morris
Mu Morris-Jones
Tina Moskal
Belinda Murphy
Marlèn Nolta
Geraldine Outhwaite
Hilary Paynter
Ivy Pedley
Suzanne Perkins
Anna Pohl
Sarah Pooley
Viv Quillin
Fiona Scott
Robin Shaw
Jackie Smith
Judy Stevens
Kate Taylor
Siân Thomas
Sandra Warne
Sarah Webb
Willow
Tamsin Wilton
Elizabeth Winkler
Paula Youens

Paula Youens and Suzanne Perkins (editors)

Women Draw 1984

The Women's Press

First published by The Women's Press Limited 1983
A member of the Namara Group
124 Shoreditch High Street, London E1 6JE

Introduction and collection ©copyright 1983
by Suzanne Perkins and Paula Youens

The copyright in each of the cartoons and drawings
in this volume remains with the original copyright
holder. No part of any work in this collection may
be reproduced without permission first being obtained
of the artist in care of the editors.

British Library Cataloguing in Publication Data

Women draw 1984
I. English wit and humour, Pictorial
I. Title II. Perkins, Suzanne
III. Youens, Paula
741.5'942 NO1476

ISBN 0-7043-3919-6

Printed and bound in Great Britain
by Mackays of Chatham Limited, Kent

Suzanne Perkins

Foreword

Although some women's cartoons are strongly in evidence, to the enjoyment of us all, I was sure there must be many more hidden in notebooks and portfolios, published in local newsletters, pinned on the wall or even waiting for the right moment to be put on paper. Why not a book drawing in talent from new sources as well as from established cartoonists?

Paula Youens, a cartoonist, and an enthusiastic watcher of cartoonists from all over the world, was keen to join me in the project.

We threw out an invitation through the press, and by word of mouth, for women to send their hopes, fears and fantasies for 1984.

First a trickle, then a flood of parcels arrived. It was an amazing experience to open them all, to read the letters that came with some of them, and to see the variety of the drawings, and the ideas they expressed.

Women Draw 1984 contains the work of 66 artists from Britain and abroad, chosen by Paula and myself, after much agonising, from hundreds. I have also included some recent drawings of Paula's.

We both hope you enjoy it, and would like to thank everyone who sent their work.

Suzanne Perkins

Women Draw 1984

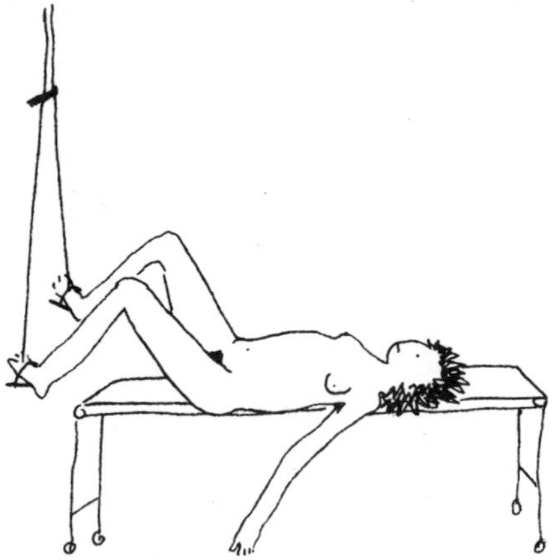

CAME
Alison McEwan

Doctor, doctor

Angela Martin

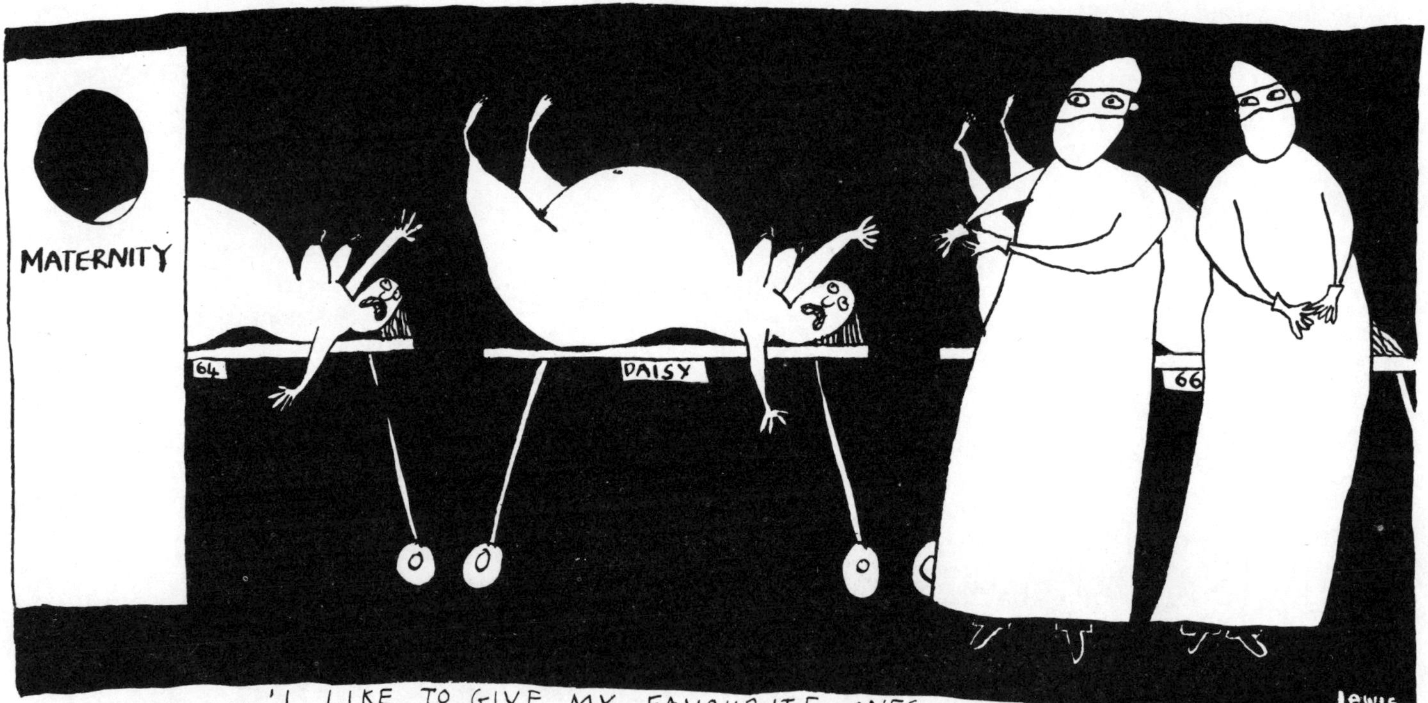

....'I LIKE TO GIVE MY FAVOURITE ONES NAMES'

Jan Lewis

Elizabeth Winkler

Helen Chadwick

Mrs Johnson was depressed.

So she stood on her head

and all her depressed bits fell out onto the floor

Mishelle Jones

Jo Harvatt

Home notes

Ironing a duvet

Angela Martin

Carey Bennet

Hilary Paynter

Sarah Webb

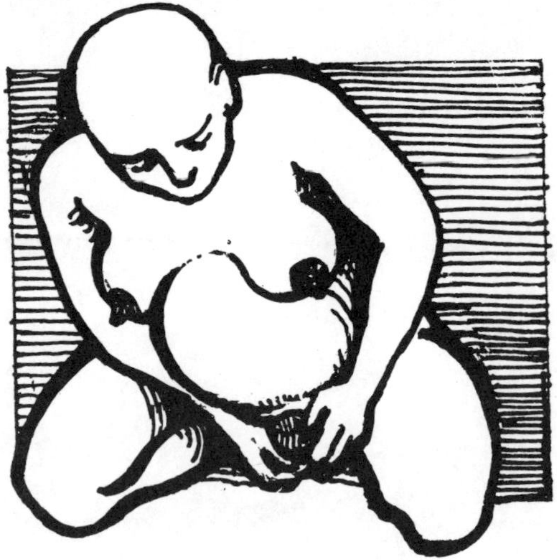
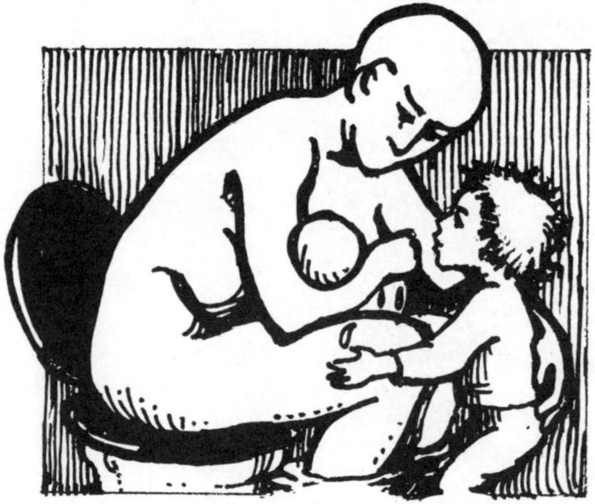
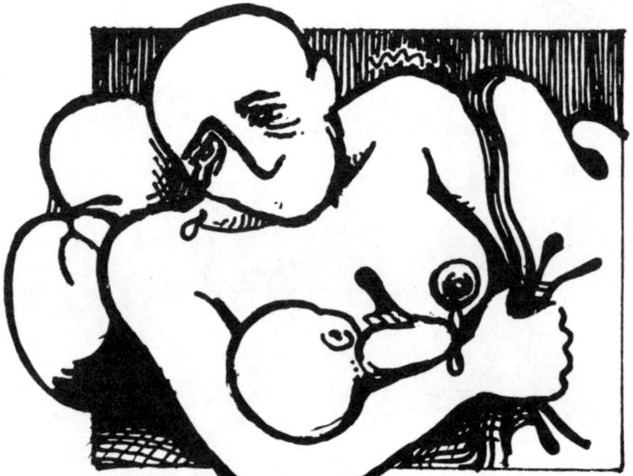

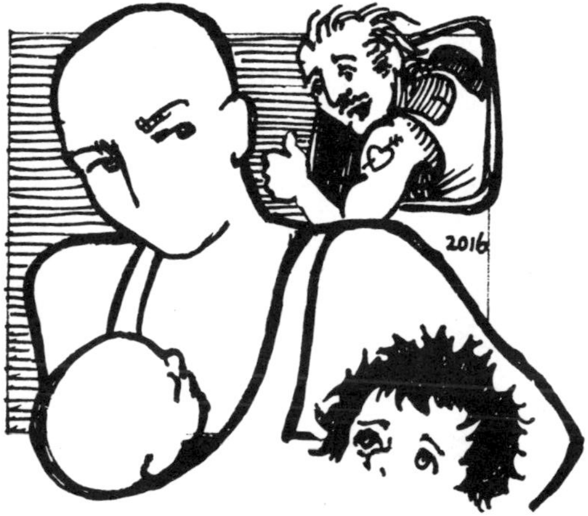

Annalou

Kathryn Lamb

Julie Hoehn

Laetitia Bermejo

IF I SEE ONE MORE CARTOON ABOUT WOMEN BEING VICTIMS OF DOMESTICITY, AND CHAINED TO THE KITCHEN SINK, I'LL SCREAM! I MEAN LIFE JUST ISN'T LIKE THAT ANYMORE
GRUDIAN

Ros Asquith

Winning bread

Viv Quillin

TCHA! THIS SEX DISCRIMINATION ACT! STUPID IDEA - CANT HAVE WOMEN BRICKLAYERS CAN YOU?
STANDS TO REASON - THEY WOULDN'T BE STRONG ENOUGH!

Jo Harvatt

Cath Jackson

Marie-Hélène Jeeves
Julie Hoehn

ONE JUST CANT BRING ONESELF TO GET UP THIS MORNING.
I WAS SUPPOSED TO HAVE BEEN UP HALF AN HOUR AGO TO SIGN ON. WHY DIDN'T YOU WAKE ME UP... EH!
SHAKE
SHAKE
YAWN
REJECT
STRETCH
DO YOU KNOW THAT WHEN YOU'VE BEEN OUT OF WORK OVER A YEAR YOU ARE TERMED "ONE OF THE HARD CORE UNEMPLO--YED"?
REJECT
I'VE BEEN SIGNING ON FOR AS LONG AS I CAN REMEMBER

Jackie Smith

· DEADLINE ·

Paula Youe

Alone, together

Helen Chadwick

Belinda Murphy

Sophie Grillet

Belinda Murphy

Annie Lawson

—A singular Life—

Some lucky man should snap you up! ...
I couldn't survive without my Keith now...
well, he's working abroad at the moment...
Monty y'know, this one's popping out soon...
THE
Life's sooo busy, I just don't have time to think about myself!

Why don't I call you when Keith gets back? We'll introduce you to one or two of his bachelor friends...
Must'nt forget old friends now, must we?
Byeee
...newfound feelings of PERFECT PEACE and CONTENTMENT
© Maggie Ling

Maggie Ling

1.
2.
3.
4
5.
I'm not sure I'd say 'celibate'.........
SB.

MAKING THINGS COMPLICATED.
I want to mention.....
...the fact that...
er, lately I've....er...
been feeling very
attracted to you!
?
!
SB.

Sue Beasley

On the eve of the conference

(or some answers to the question – what do we actually <u>do</u> in bed?)

Drink tea . . .

knit . . . . .

gossip about friends . . .

read the newsletter . . . .

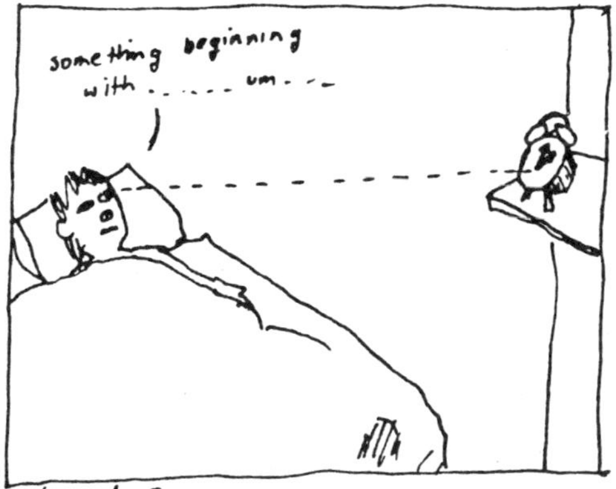

play I-spy _ _

blow bubbles _ _ _

(Blank space for anything I've left out) fill it in yourself.

sleep.

Name mislaid. Apologies.

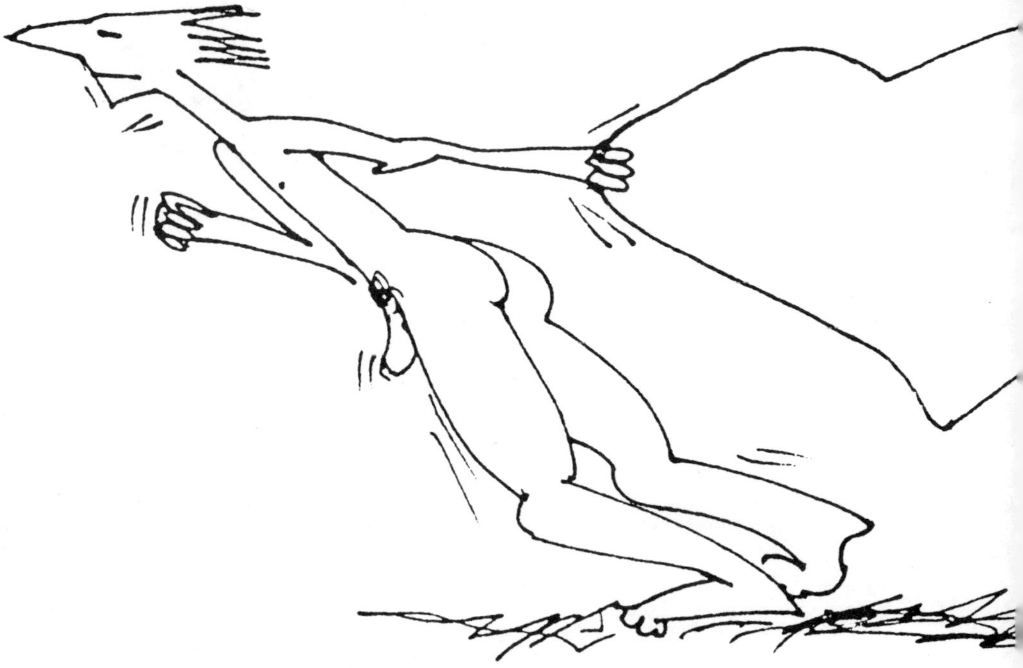

Robin Shaw

Kate Charlsworth

Paloma Massip-Pozo

Struggle and strife

shit...

god why didn't
I think of that?

present

Jacky Fleming

LUST

ANGER

Carel Moiseiwitsch
Ros Asquith
Sandra Warne

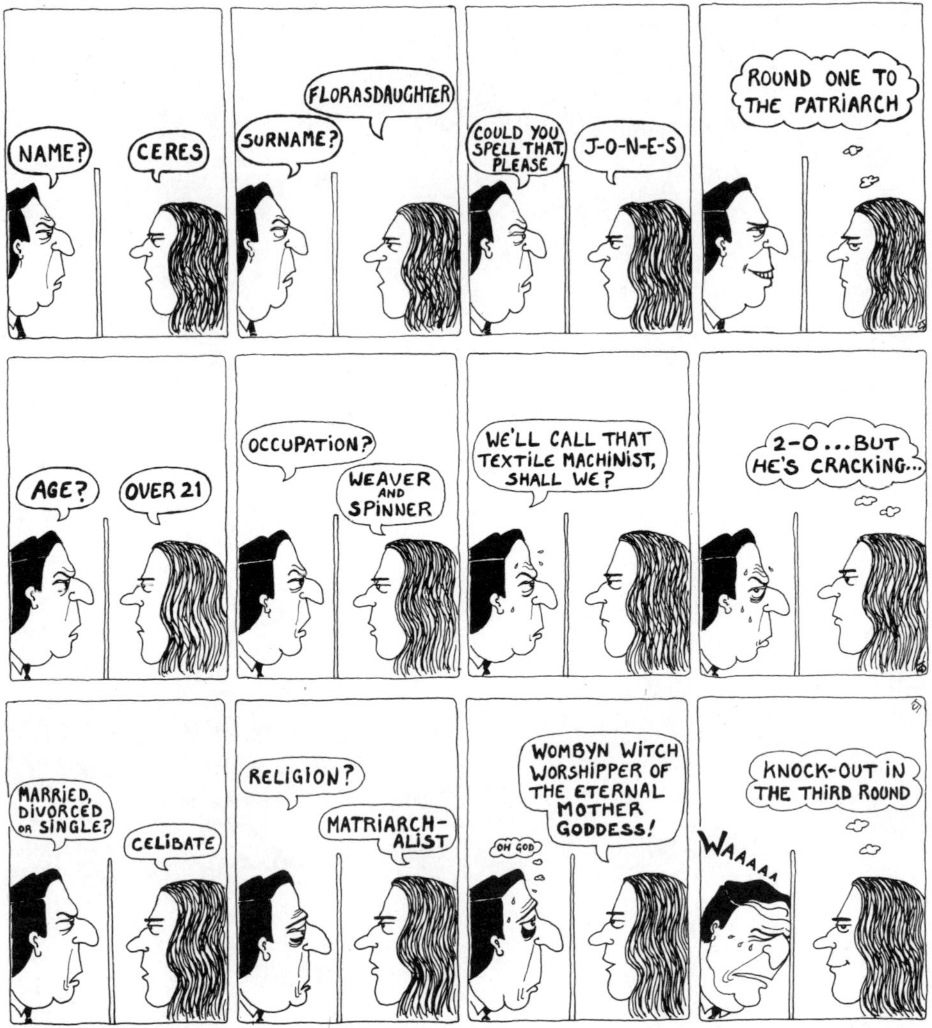

Cath Jackson

Sally Corless

Belinda Murphy

Linda Harding

Jean Meyer

LAWS ARE MADE TO BE BROKEN

Sarah Webb

Ann Barefoot

just reforming the trade union laws
My hero
Just questioning the powers that be
POLICE

Marian Lydbrooke

Annie Lawson

Marlèn Nolta

DO NOT ADJUST YOUR SET
OOPS, SORRY, THAT WAS A SLIP OF THE TONGUE I'M AFRAID ...
NOLTA '83 ©

THINK
-DUH-
-ER-
WELL
-ER-
HM GOVT. THINK TANK
♫
HMMM...
(YAWN)

Anna Pohl

Underneath ~ they're all Lovable . . .

Tamsin Wilton

Paula Youens

War, war, war

Helen Cherry

HAIRSTYLE FOR '84
THE 'NUCLEAR BOMBE SURPRISE'

Riana Duncan
Kathryn Lamb

Fiona Scott

How To Survive the Bomb .....

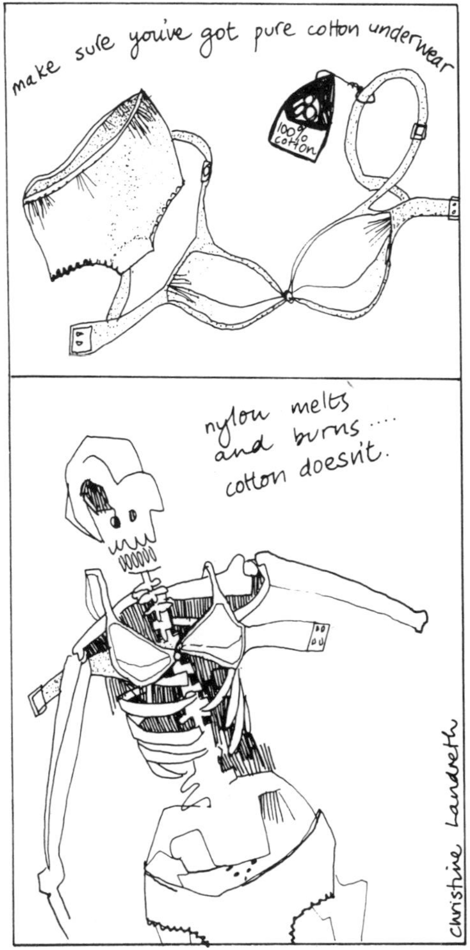

Christine Landreth

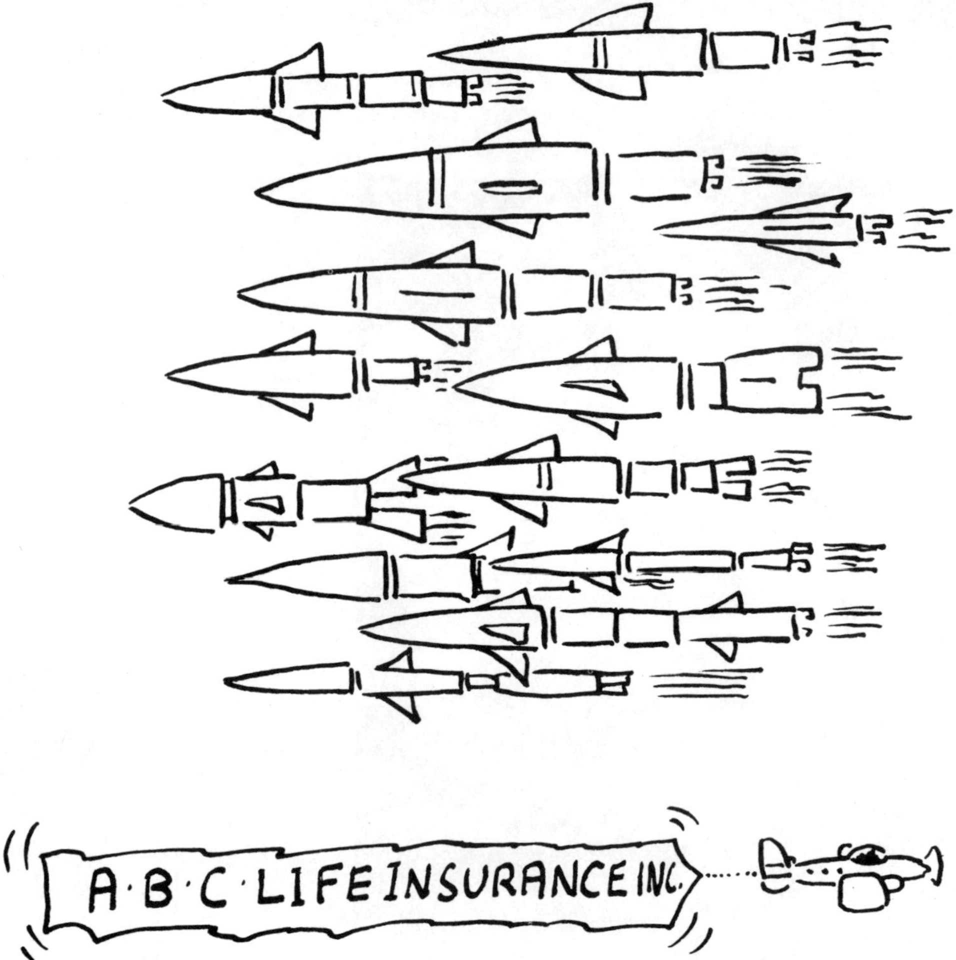

Stefy Morris

One day my son all this will be — oh, forget it!

:efy Morris

ıula Youens

ıarie-Hélène Jeeves

OH WHAT A BEAUTIFUL DAY!
UTOPIA!
HOLOCAUST!

UTOPIA... HOLOCAUST... UTOPIA... HOLOCAUST... UTOPIA..HOLOCAUST UTOPIAHOLOCAUST UTOPIAHOLOCAUST UTOPIA... HOLOCAUST...
UTOPIA!!
WELL... WHEN ITS YOUR FUTURE AT STAKE, YOU'RE JUSTIFIED IN CHEATING A LITTLE... SURELY!
WILLOW

Willow

Paula Youens

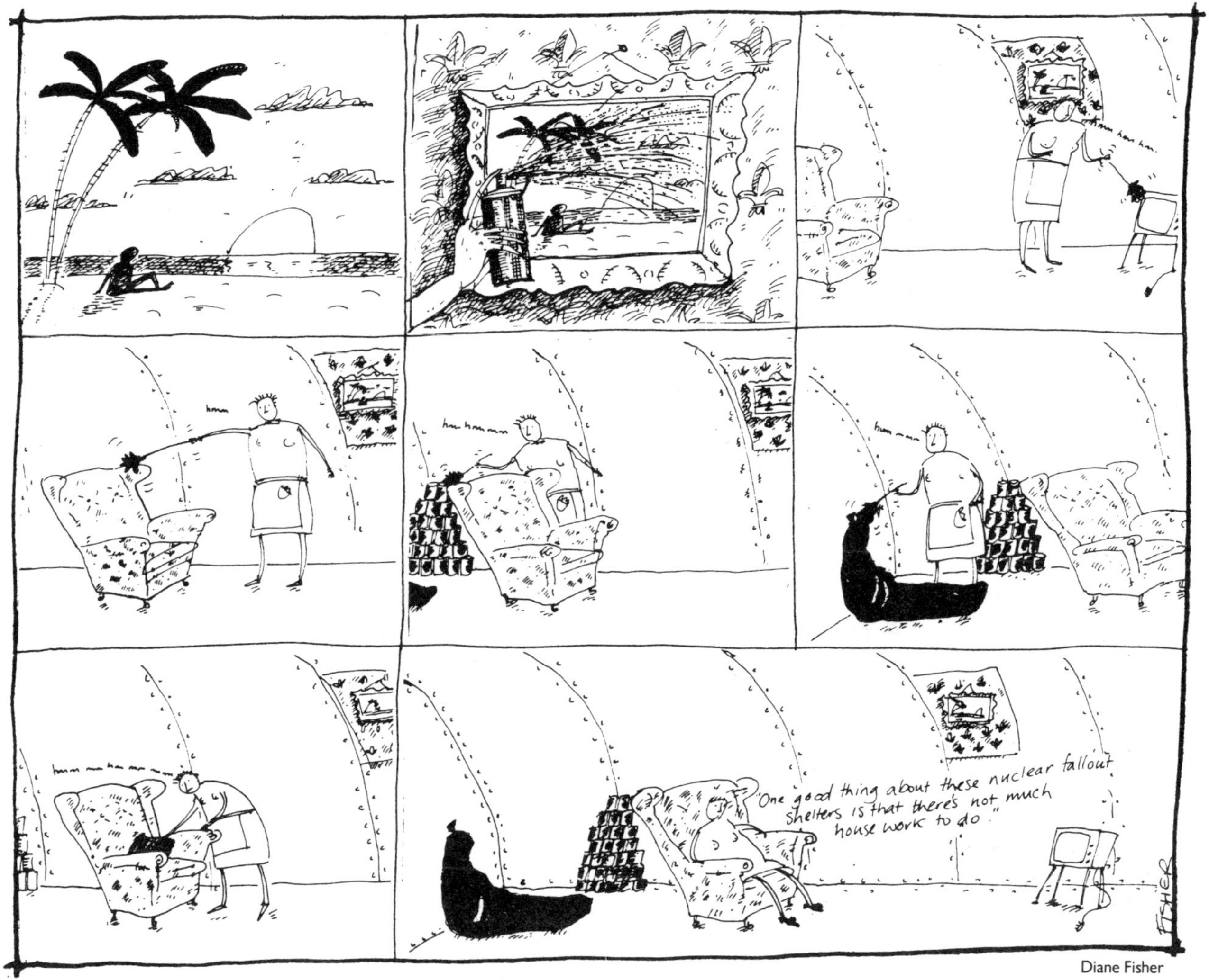

Diane Fisher

Judy Stevens

Progress!

Wanda Gorzgowska

COULD THIS BE THE END OF SEXISM AS WE KNOW IT ?!!
...

OR ONLY THE BEGINNING!

Siân Thomas

*Hello house, switch on heating, defrost moussaka, start laundromat —
and look, I'm sorry about this morning, I clean forgot it was your birthday —*

Margaret Maidment

'But I'm still lonely at nights!'

Bridget Moore
Geraldine Outhwaite

Mary Ellis

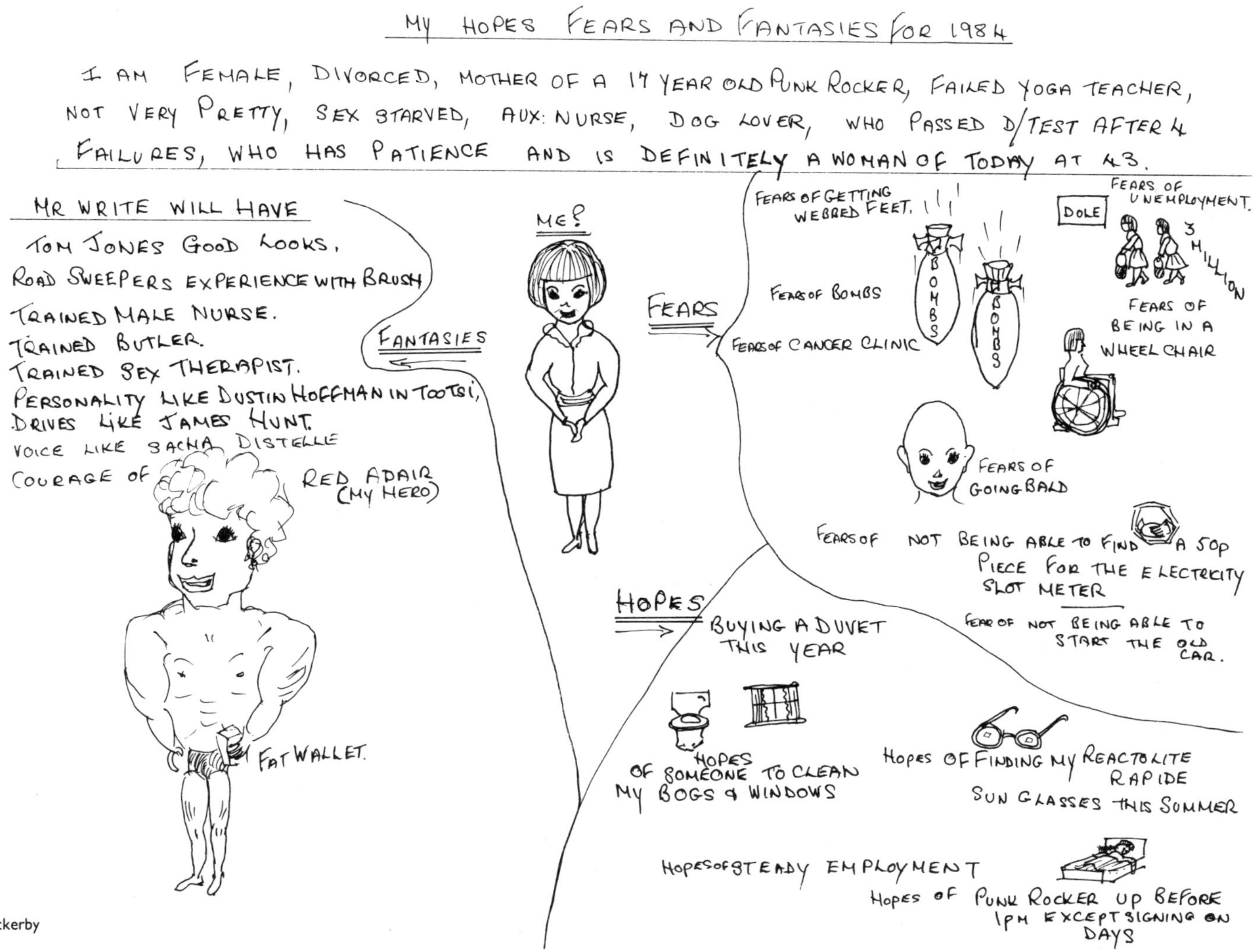

June Huckerby

Carel Moiseiwitsch

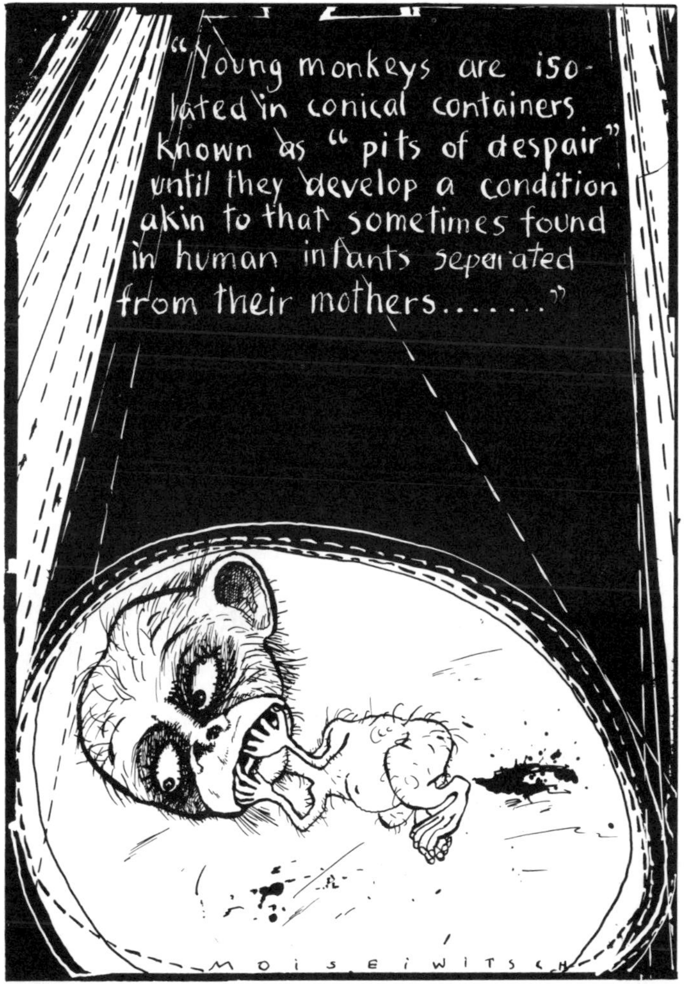

Carel Moiseiwitsch

Sarah Pooley

Body politics

Sue Beasley
Kate Taylor
Ann Barefoot
Angela Martin
Julie Hoehn
Naomi Alexander

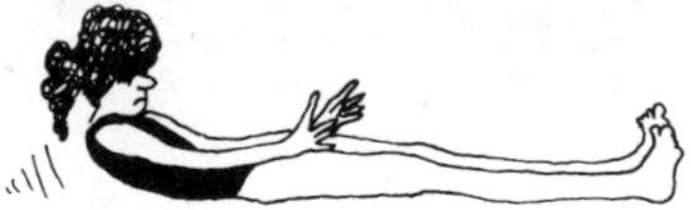

Beastly boobs....
horrid hams....
BAD bottom!
FOUL, FOUL FLESH!
IT'S ALL YOUR FAULT!!
!
!
Tina
I'm sorry! I'm sorry! I didn't mean it!

Tina M.

Tina Moskal

Mu Morris-Jones

Paula Youens

Jackie Smith

Sophie Grillet

Ivy Pedley

Naomi Alexander

Life in general...

Hilary Driver

A MARRIAGE OF CONVENIENCE...

Caroline Holden

Cath Jackson

Lyn May

Annie Lawson

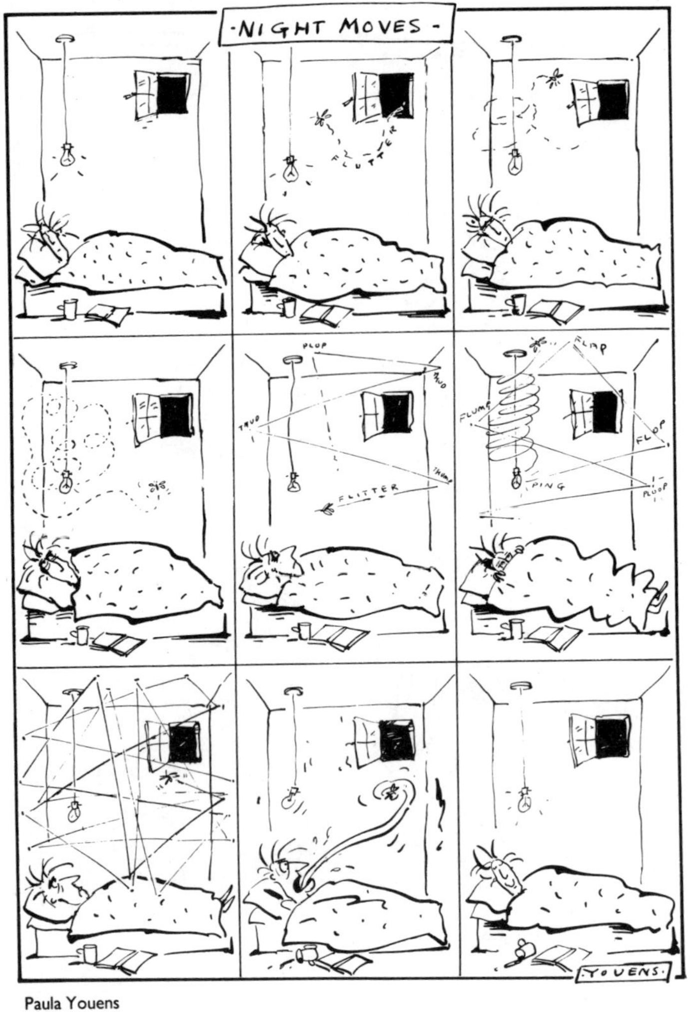

Paula Youens

Laetitia Bermejo

Annie Lawson

FRANJOOLIES

Well, isn't this great? Here we are enjoying Nature at her best. I don't know why people cut themselves off from the beautiful, healthy bounty of Nature...
...when they could be out here enjoying the elements, breathing the sharp, clean air, and partaking of the Great Outdoors, like us.
Don't worry, dear. I'm sure it will stop raining tomorrow...
d'Arcy©

Renée d'Arcy

Belinda Murphy

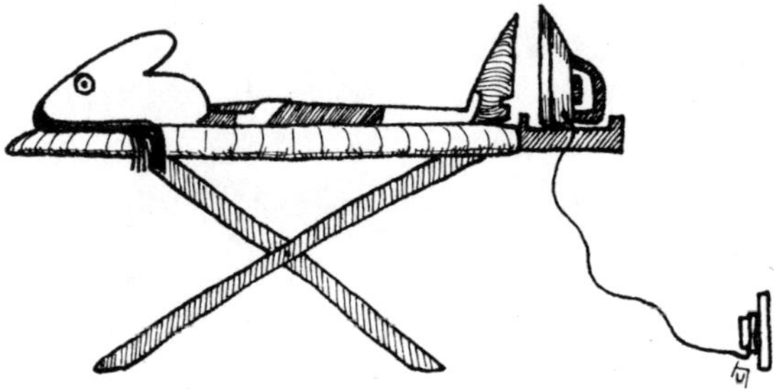

Cath Jackson